CANOEING

CANOEING

ODYSSEYS

JOY FRISCH-SCHMOLL

🍎 CREATIVE EDUCATION

Published by Creative Education
P.O. Box 227, Mankato, Minnesota 56002
Creative Education is an imprint of The Creative Company
www.thecreativecompany.us

Design by Blue Design (www.bluedes.com)
Production by Joe Kahnke
Art direction by Rita Marshall
Printed in China

Photographs by Alamy (aaronpeterson.net, All Canada
Photos, Design Pics Inc., epa european pressphoto agency b.v.,
Michele Molinari, Outdoor-Archiv, Profimedia.CZ a.s.), Creative
Commons Wikimedia (Real Landry), Dreamstime (Elena
Elisseeva), Flickr (joeldinda), Getty Images (Thomas Barwick,
Gustave Caillebotte, Henry Georgi, Liysa), iStockphoto (ajlber,
shalamov, Cameron Strathdee), NWWoodsman.com (Yevette
Neilsen), River Sports Magazine (Quebec Winter Carnival),
Shutterstock (Dudarev Mikhail, Smileus, Ivan Smuk)

Image on p. 75 courtesy of Dana Starkell; it first appeared in
the *Winnipeg Free Press* and later in the book *Paddle to the
Amazon*.

Library of Congress Cataloging-in-Publication Data
Names: Frisch-Schmoll, Joy, author.
Title: Canoeing / Joy Frisch-Schmoll.
Series: Odysseys in outdoor adventures.
Includes bibliographical references, webography, and index.
Summary: An in-depth survey of the history of canoeing, as
well as tips and advice on how to choose a canoe, how to
prepare for a trip, and the skills and supplies necessary for
different types of canoeing.
Identifiers: LCCN 2016031800 / ISBN 978-1-60818-686-0
(hardcover) / ISBN 978-1-56660-722-3 (eBook)

Subjects: LCSH: 1. Canoes and canoeing—Juvenile literature.
2. Canoes and canoeing—History—Juvenile literature.
Classification: LCC GV784.3.F75 2017 / DDC 797.122—dc23

CCSS: RI.7.1, 2, 3, 4, 5; RI.8.1, 2, 3, 4, 5; RI.9-10.1, 2, 3, 4; RI.11-12.1,
2, 3, 4; RH.6-8.1, 2, 4, 5; RH.9-10.2, 4, 5

First Edition 9 8 7 6 5 4 3 2 1

CONTENTS

Introduction

Adventure awaits! It's a call from Mother Nature heard by nature lovers and thrill seekers alike. This temptation beckons them, prompting them to pack their gear, pull on their jackets, and head out the door. From mountain peaks to ocean depths and everything in between, the earth is a giant playground for those who love to explore and challenge themselves. Not content to follow the beaten

OPPOSITE: Whether on a quiet lake or a rushing river, canoeing is a good way to appreciate the beauty and natural power of your surroundings.

path, they push the limits by venturing farther, faster, deeper, and higher. Going to such lengths, they discover satisfaction, excitement, and fun. Theirs is a world of thrilling outdoor adventures.

Canoeing is one such adventure. Although exploring a narrow stream or gliding across a small pond can be quiet and relaxing, other canoe trips can be wild rides. Whether taking a multi-day trip into the wilderness, tackling whitewater rapids, or racing in flat-water competitions, canoe paddlesports offer as much excitement as a person desires. In some places, canoes are the only means of accessing remote areas, allowing paddlers to get up close to nature. Although the canoe has always been a simple boat, advances in materials and design now allow enthusiasts to use it in increasingly extreme ways.

Canoeing through History

Boats are an ancient form of transportation. People the world over have been making and using canoes for thousands of years. The first style of canoe was the dugout, a primitive, simple watercraft formed by hollowing out a single tree log. The Pesse canoe, found in the Netherlands, is believed to be the world's oldest known boat.

OPPOSITE Ancient peoples used hardwood trees to make a dugout canoe. First, they removed the bark. Then, they set fires on the top of the log to hollow it out. People today still follow a similar process.

Using the technique of carbon dating, scientists have determined that it was constructed sometime between 8200 and 7600 B.C. The Dufuna canoe, another dugout, is Africa's oldest boat. It is more than 8,000 years old.

The solid dugouts were made from long, straight tree trunks. Using sharp rocks and antlers, ancient people hollowed out the logs, creating a sitting area. Sometimes they used fire to burn a hole in the center. Then they shaped and smoothed the outside. These heavy vessels served an important role in the lives of early humans for hunting, fishing, and transportation. Impractical to carry overland, they were often left behind when paddlers arrived at their destination. In the Caribbean, native peoples used log boats to travel from island to island.

On the North American mainland, a different type of canoe had a frame structure. Made of strong pieces of wood, the lightweight frame was covered with materials specific to particular regions. American Indians in the north stretched bark or the hides of animals such as moose or caribou over the wooden frames. In the east, birch or elm bark was used. The pieces of tree bark were stitched together and glued into place. With plenty of space inside, these open boats served many purposes in early peoples' daily lives. They fished and gathered food from lakes and streams. Canoes were also used for traveling, hunting, trading with neighboring people, and fighting wars.

When Europeans came to North America, they adopted the canoe as well. Modeled after the natives' boats, their large freight canoes could hold up to 12 people. French-Canadian trappers called voyageurs transported trading goods and furs from the forests out to trading posts. As these explorers and traders navigated rivers and rapids in their birchbark canoes, they exposed the New World to European-style commerce and trade. They opened up much of the country to exploration

before there were any roads. Canoe routes became like today's highways. Other people followed the trails of early explorers, and cities were founded along the waterways.

For much of its history, the canoe was a working boat. But with the invention of trains, paddling for transportation was no longer necessary or practical. In the mid-1800s, the focus shifted to paddling for recreation. People studied the boats of natives and developed their own designs. Construction materials changed to canvas on a wood frame. Canoeing took on a whole new purpose: enjoyment.

A Scottish lawyer and adventurer named John MacGregor (1825–92) is credited with popularizing canoeing in Europe and the United States. After designing a boat he called the "Rob Roy," MacGregor spent the next several years exploring waterways of Europe and the Middle East.

He wrote books and gave lectures about his adventures and founded the British Royal Canoe Club in 1866 to develop the sport. The club held its first regatta—a series of boat races involving rowed watercraft—that year. The New York Canoe Club was founded five years later, piggybacking on the success of the Royal Canoe Club.

In the U.S., recreational canoeing continued to grow in popularity during the early 1900s. Young couples enjoyed leisurely paddling dates as part of the "canoe craze." They would accessorize their canoes with pillows, lanterns, and picnicking supplies for a day on the water. Some even customized their canoes with built-in record players to play music. Flat-water racing was introduced as a demonstration sport at the 1924 Olympics and became an official event in the 1936 Games. Construction materials evolved after World War II, when the Grumman Aircraft Engineering Corporation began producing aluminum canoes.

Across North America, canoeing was promoted by numerous people as a recreational activity and as a way to encounter and appreciate nature. American author and environmentalist Sigurd F. Olson (1899–1982) worked to promote and protect wilderness areas. He helped establish the Boundary Waters Canoe Area Wilderness (BWCAW) in northern Minnesota, the world's most famous canoe country. For more than 30 years, he served as a wilderness guide, leading canoe expeditions.

During his lifetime, adventurer Verlen Kruger (1922–2004) paddled more than 100,000 miles (160,934 km). That is the most of anyone in the sport and more than four times the distance around the earth!

Another author named Bill Mason (1929–88) was a canoe expert and Canadian naturalist. Known primarily for his books, films, and art, Mason developed canoeing strokes and river-running techniques, especially for whitewater situations.

I n some ways, canoeing has changed little since prehistoric times. Today's canoes are similar in overall design to the ones American Indians used for centuries. But a closer inspection reveals some differences. Canoes have increasingly been made from lighter materials, which have improved their durability and ease of transport. Today, canoes are made from aluminum, fiberglass, and a combination of other materials such as vinyl, plastic, and foam. Kevlar is a strong and lightweight synthetic fiber commonly used in canoe construction. Advances in materials and style have enabled canoeing to evolve into the activity it is today.

The kinds of canoeing are just as varied as the materials and designs. People take their boats where they never before would have dared. There is a perfectly designed canoe for whatever kind of paddling a person chooses.

Advances in materials and style have enabled canoeing to evolve into the recreational and sporting activity it is today.

There are fast ones and slow ones, wide ones and skinny ones, short ones and long ones. A recreational canoeist can enjoy a chilled-out afternoon on the lake. Someone interested in extended trips can load a canoe with gear and take off for a week or more. Thrill seekers can gravitate toward whitewater paddling and playboating, a modern type of canoeing where paddlers perform various technical moves. Those eager to compete can participate in many racing events. Today, paddling can be for fun, exercise, competition, or adventure. From peaceful paddling to tricks and stunts, there is something for everyone.

Know Your Boat

Regardless of design, all canoes share the same basic components. Match the parts to where they belong.

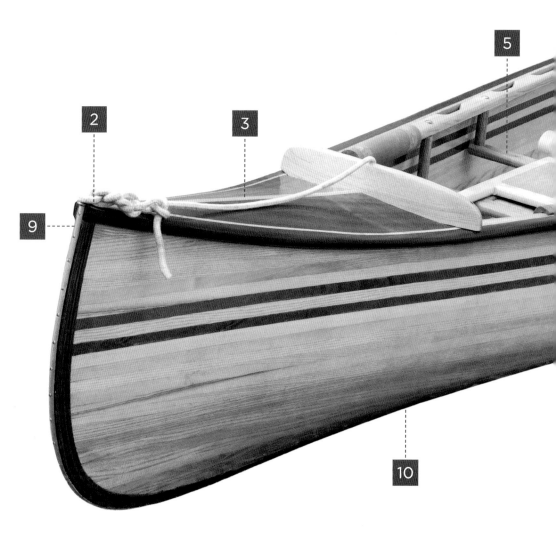

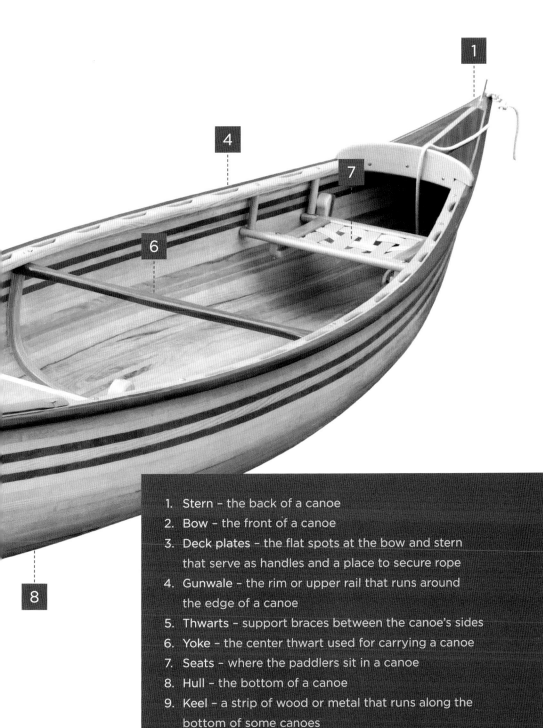

1. Stern – the back of a canoe
2. Bow – the front of a canoe
3. Deck plates – the flat spots at the bow and stern
   that serve as handles and a place to secure rope
4. Gunwale – the rim or upper rail that runs around
   the edge of a canoe
5. Thwarts – support braces between the canoe's sides
6. Yoke – the center thwart used for carrying a canoe
7. Seats – where the paddlers sit in a canoe
8. Hull – the bottom of a canoe
9. Keel – a strip of wood or metal that runs along the
   bottom of some canoes
10. Rocker – the upward curve of the hull along the
    keel from the bow to the stern

Grab Your Paddle

The various kinds of canoeing share similarities, but they also differ in equipment and technique. The canoes themselves are uniquely shaped for each activity. The hull of a canoe, for example, affects the boat's speed and how easily it steers. The hull's shape also affects how stable the canoe is. Recreational canoeing is best done with a long, steady boat with a flat hull. With plenty of space for people and gear, a flat-hulled canoe is

OPPOSITE: For a pleasant day of paddling, make sure you have the right gear. Sunscreen, sunglasses, and a helmet or brimmed hat are important on sunny days. Always wear a life jacket wherever you go.

easy to paddle on calm water. Canoeists who want to go faster use canoes with rounded bottoms. These canoes are better suited to experienced canoeists because the boats are unsteady. Racers use long, skinny canoes with V-shaped hulls. These are the easiest to paddle in a straight line and move easily through the water, giving racers the necessary speed.

Once the perfect canoe is chosen, it's time to select the next item: the paddle. Like canoes, paddles come in many styles. Regardless of other design

Long, skinny canoes cut through the water easily and are perfect vessels for racing.

Ready to Launch

Getting into a canoe doesn't have to be tricky. With a little practice, launching can be smooth and easy. Your canoe should be floating flat on water that is deep enough to prevent the boat from getting stuck after loading. Place the paddles on the bottom of the canoe and stow your gear. If launching with a partner, the other person will steady the canoe as you get in. Grab the gunwales with both hands and step into the middle of the boat. Stay low and keep your weight centered as you walk carefully to your seat. Lower yourself into a seated or kneeling position and pick up your paddle. After your partner is in and settled, gently push off. Now you can start paddling!

If a paddle is too small, it loses paddling power. If it is too heavy, it can be difficult and tiring to use.

features, all canoe paddles have a single blade at the bottom and a handle to grip at the top. Paddle blades and lengths differ according to their intended function. Some have long, rounded blades, while others are wider and shorter. Some have a squared-off end. Some are designed to move lots of water in one stroke for quick maneuvers. The goal is to find the paddle with the right balance of strength, weight, and power. If a paddle is too small, it loses paddling power. If it is too heavy, it can be difficult and tiring to use. The best paddles are light and very strong. Paddles are made from a variety of materials, including plastic, fiberglass, light metal, and wood.

To paddle, you rotate your torso from side to side, taking strokes on opposite sides of a canoe. When tandem canoeing, where two people work together as a team, each person takes turns paddling on each side. The person in the stern does the steering by using the paddle as a rudder, while the person in the bow often sets the pace. Paddling can be done from a seated or kneeling position. Although most canoes have seats, some people prefer kneeling because it gives them greater control and keeps the canoe stabler by lowering and distributing their weight. Kneeling provides better leverage and power, and it is especially helpful in windy conditions or when shooting rapids.

For beginners, a few basic strokes are essential to learn. The forward stroke propels the canoe forward in a straight line. It is done by putting the blade of the paddle in the water at a right angle to the canoe, and then pulling back on the paddle while keeping it close beside the boat. The back stroke is for stopping forward movement or for going backward. To do the back stroke, you put the blade in the water and push from the back of the canoe to the front. To move sideways, a draw stroke is used, reaching the blade out in the water and pulling it toward the canoe. A pry stroke is for when you need to avoid hitting a sudden obstacle. Put the blade in the water under the canoe and push it away.

To turn or change direction, paddlers need to put in more strokes on one side of the canoe than the other. The more strokes they take on one side, the faster the boat will turn. To make a sharper turn, paddlers take a backward stroke. The boat will slow down and pivot around the paddle. Although canoes can carry several people, only one person is needed to paddle a canoe. A solo canoeist can use a J-stroke to travel in a straight line while paddling on just one side of the boat. The J-stroke is a forward stroke that ends with a quick turn of the paddle and a gentle push away from the canoe. Using this steering stroke will keep a canoe on course.

A side from a boat and a paddle, canoeists benefit from having some key pieces of gear. Everyone in a canoe needs a personal flotation device (PFD), or life jacket. It will keep a person afloat in the water if they fall out or if the canoe capsizes. The right headgear is important, too. Someone who paddles on flat, calm

water may get by with a wide-brimmed hat, but a helmet is essential for anyone who paddles in fast-moving water. Wetsuits and other waterproof clothing help keep paddlers comfortable and dry. Sunglasses protect the eyes by blocking the sun's reflection off the water. Other useful items include a **dry bag**, first aid kit, rope, and whistle.

Once a person knows how to paddle and has the necessary equipment, canoeing can be enjoyed practically year round. It is not necessarily limited by the seasons. Spring and fall may offer the most comfortable temperatures, but neither heat nor cold deters the hardiest of adventurers. As long as paddlers are prepared and dressed for the conditions, the time of year should not restrict their activities. Only completely frozen lakes and rivers prevent enthusiasts from launching their canoes. Where open water exists, gliding past icebergs and glaciers is an

option for those who have the desire and adequate warm layers of clothing. In fact, some canoeing competitions are held in the winter when semi-frozen rivers and ice chunks add to the challenge.

Most people put their canoes in storage during the winter months and wait for spring's warmer weather before they venture out. But the heat of summer can bring its own challenges, and anyone on the water should be prepared. Plenty of drinking water, sunscreen, and a hat are essentials on hot days. A bright, sunny day with calm winds may look ideal, but canoeists know to be ready for any type of weather. Being a smart boater means watching the skies for signs of storms and knowing when to get off the water.

Proceed with Caution

With any outdoor adventure or sport there are risks, but with extreme sports, there are even more. As the popularity of extreme sports has soared in recent years, so have the rates of injuries. Some people seeking an **adrenaline** rush try to copy stunts they see online or on TV. Feeling overconfident, but lacking skills and training, they put themselves in danger.

And often they fail to use safety equipment that could reduce the risk of serious injury. When risk becomes reality, broken bones, concussions, and other life-threatening injuries can happen.

Because canoeing takes people places they may not normally go, they may encounter hazardous situations. Whether in the middle of a lake, on a fast-flowing river, or even along an ocean coastline, being in an unfamiliar environment can be exciting, but it is also potentially dangerous, which is part of the appeal for some people.

However, by gaining skills and learning to manage the risks, canoeing can be the fun and rewarding activity it is meant to be.

Since coaches, referees, and medical personnel are present at sporting events, competitive canoeing activities are usually safer than noncompetitive ones. Rules are in place, safety equipment is mandatory, and participants have typically received supervised training. Although accidents and mishaps can occur even at organized events, they are less likely. It is when untrained amateurs attempt too much that serious problems and injuries usually occur.

Canoeing in wilderness areas is risky because emergency assistance may be hours away. Anyone who ventures into a remote area needs to be capable of reacting to a variety of situations. Having knowledge

Canoeists should expect to capsize occasionally and be able to swim to safety.

of basic survival skills is a must. A person should know how to read a map, administer first aid, and respond to outdoor adversities. Biting insects, severe weather, and run-ins with wildlife are possible threats. Many mishaps can occur in the wild, and a canoe outing can quickly go wrong, if people are not prepared for that environment.

Paddling through rapids, waves, or any kind of moving water presents other dangers. The power of moving water should not be underestimated. Currents can overtake even the strongest of swimmers. Canoeists should expect to capsize occasionally and be able to swim to safety. In rough water, the risk of drowning exists when getting trapped underwater is a possibility. Rocks and dams are features to avoid, as are strainers, which are objects such

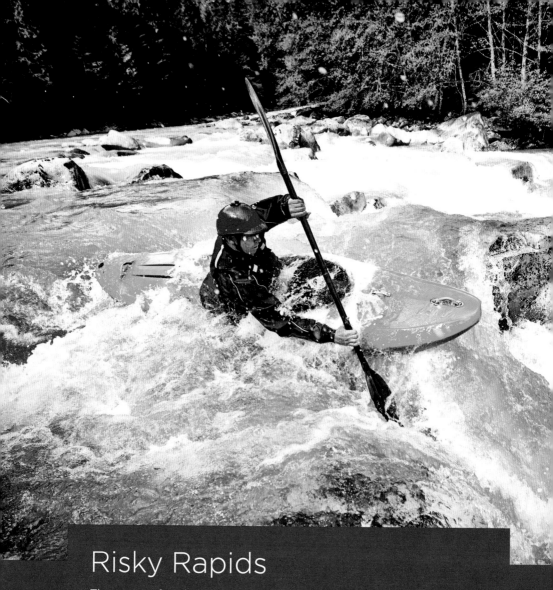

Risky Rapids

The system for classifying the level of challenge for various sections of a river is known as the International Scale of River Difficulty. Using the roman numerals I through VI, it ranges from "very easy" to "life threatening." A Class I river is easy with some small waves and few obstacles. Class II is moderate, with easily navigable small rapids and waves. Class III requires complex maneuvers. It has challenging rapids and lots of large waves. Advanced Class IV is very difficult with raging rapids that are turbulent and unpredictable. The risk of injury is significant. Class V is for experts, thanks to its extremely violent rapids, big drops, and many hazards. Class VI is too as downed trees or logs that lie in the water and can trap things underneath them. A person can reduce the risk of serious injury by using proper safety equipment such as life jackets and helmets. These items have saved many lives and helped prevent many serious head injuries.

Cold water is extremely dangerous—even deadly. Immersion in cold water is the most serious threat to an unprepared paddler. Even on a hot day, the water can still be chilly. Being cold, wet, and miserable can ruin a canoe outing. Staying warm and dry inside a wetsuit and other layers protects paddlers from the cold. Without such clothing, they risk **hypothermia**. Almost as dangerous as the cold is the heat from the sun. Paddlers need to take precautions to avoid the pain of sunburn. Dehydration and sunstroke are both serious conditions that can leave a person feeling weak and dizzy.

Before heading out on the water, paddlers should assess the conditions and know the difficulty ratings of any rivers they will be on. This means knowing the natural hazards of the journey and being confident that everyone can cope with the challenges. It is best to err on the side of caution. To avoid capsizing or **swamping**, paddlers sometimes need to scout rapids from land and portage around them. Portaging involves carrying a canoe and its gear over land from one body of water to another.

Highly skilled experts are able to take greater chances

on the water and remain safe. In an extreme move, Canadian Jim Coffey made whitewater history in November 2013 when he paddled his **open canoe** over the edge of a 60-foot (18.3 m) waterfall in Mexico. In doing so, he broke the world canoe waterfall record of 55 feet (16.8 m) that had stood for 20 years. His fame was short-lived, however, because his record was broken only a few months later. The viral video of Coffey's stunt inspired daredevil Brad McMillan to see if he could do better. In April 2014, McMillan successfully ran the 70-foot (21.3 m) Desoto Falls in Alabama.

Breaking records and performing stunts can be thrilling, but canoes can also be used for other purposes. Some people use them as vehicles for community projects and conservation efforts. Across the country, there are various organizations that work to restore and protect the health of rivers, streams, lakes, and wetlands. For example, Paddle Without Pollution and Canoes for a Cause are two groups that work to clean up America's polluted waterways. Volunteers remove litter and illegally dumped waste from rivers, creeks, and lakes. In canoes, they are able to access shallow and other hard-to-reach areas.

Overall, canoeing is an environmentally friendly, "green" activity. It has very little negative impact on the environment, unlike motorboats, which cause noise and pollution. There are no fast-moving blades on a canoe to

Will a concrete canoe float? Yes! Each year, engineering students from North American universities compete to build the best concrete canoe. Then they race each other on a flat-water course.

cause damage to fish or other marine wildlife. As long as the people in the canoes respect nature and act responsibly, canoeing does not contribute to any environmental concerns. In fact, it can be used to raise awareness and improve the environment.

Responsible boaters leave no trace of their visit and take their litter home with them. They leave their surroundings as they found them. To avoid damaging vegetation when launching or landing, they lift rather than drag their canoes. Showing respect for the environment means caring not only about the water but also about the land, plants, and wildlife. Canoeing is at its best when everyone can safely enjoy being on the water and the environment does not suffer because of it.

Today's Canoeing Culture

In places such as the U.S. and Canada, where it played an important historical role, the canoe remains popular in the wider culture. In our society today, canoeing is as varied as the individuals who pursue it. It can be an expedition trip, a ride on thundering rapids, a show of tricks, or a grueling race. From mild to wild, canoeing covers a range of levels. Finding the perfect niche depends on one's preferences and abilities. Canoeing can bring relaxation or challenge a paddler's strength and quicken her pulse in an all-out physical effort.

Although canoeing can be done on nearly any lake close to you, certain regions offer especially wonderful paddling opportunities. Exploring the swampy Everglades in Florida will be much different from traversing the expansive Great Lakes of the north. And from Alaska's icy waters to the Colorado River's whitewater

Paddler's Paradise

For canoe enthusiasts seeking the ultimate paddling experience of unspoiled nature and solitude, the Boundary Waters Canoe Area Wilderness (BWCAW) is a dream come true. Located in northeastern Minnesota just south of the Ontario border, the BWCAW is approximately 1.1 million acres (441,075 ha) in size. With a thousand sparkling lakes and streams, it offers more than 1,200 miles (1,931 km) of canoe routes and 2,000-plus sites for overnight campers. It is a place where canoes rule the water. Paddlers can enjoy the wilderness in much the same way that French voyageurs did 200 years ago. There are no motors, no electricity, no telephone lines, and no roads to the inner lakes. Each year, this legendary destination receives more than rapids, the possibilities of river canoeing are abundant. These locations and many others have outfitters that set up paddlers with the canoes, paddles, and gear needed for a day on the water.

Canoeing is tied to tourism in many locations across the U.S. Tour companies assist with trip planning and lead on-the-water tours. In some areas, charter planes and boats are available to deliver canoeists to remote locations. With thousands of miles of lakeshores and rivers to explore, there is no shortage of options for enthusiasts. The hardest part may be deciding where to go and in what type of canoeing to partake!

For many people, paddling on flat, open water is the classic way to enjoy canoeing. It is perfect for beginners as well as veterans of the sport. In the seats of a canoe, paddlers can leave their busy lives behind and escape into wild locations for some peace and solitude. Many paddlers use canoes to partake in another favorite outdoor activity: camping. They fill their canoes with supplies, food, and shelter. Multi-day trips bring challenges but also great rewards, such as beautiful scenery and thrilling wildlife viewing. In northern regions, canoeists may see moose, deer, bears, foxes, and beavers. In the South, crocodiles, manatees, and tropical birds may be spotted. Seals and dolphins commonly share the waters with paddlers along the coasts.

To feel adrenaline coursing through their veins, advanced paddlers prefer whitewater canoeing, which can mean anything from gently rolling waters to severe rapids and dangerous drops. Kayaks are more typical choices, but open canoes can also be used. Whitewater paddlers often fill their canoes with air bags to keep out water and help their boats stay light. Whether river running as part of a race or a scenic tour, canoeists need strong nerves, experience, and skill. Whitewater canoeing is an exhilarating adventure of steering around boulders, tackling waterfalls, and experiencing the raw power of nature.

A modern form of canoeing called playboating has an emphasis on style. In specialized canoes known as playboats or squirt boats, participants perform a series of acrobatic moves. They spin, surf, turn, and flip in one place called a playspot. Sometimes they even

become airborne. Playboating is mainly done for fun, but competitions known as freestyle are also popular. Paddlers have a set time to perform as many tricks and moves as they can. They can also score additional points for style.

For expressive canoeists who prefer a calmer, more serene stage, there is free-style canoe dance. This unique form of canoeing is done on flat, still water. Paddle strokes are performed in a deliberate, graceful way. Performances are set to music and demonstrate fancy paddle work and precise boat control. From a kneeling position, participants work the paddle to make their canoes spin, go sideways and backward, and do figure eights and spirals. By paddling and leaning this way and that to redistribute their weight, performers can make their canoes appear to be dancing. Competitors are judged on choreography (the sequence of movements), creativity, showmanship, and paddle technique.

The pinnacle of canoe competition occurs every four years at the Summer Olympics, where there are the two canoeing events: the sprint and the slalom. The sprint is all about speed. Held on flat water, it is a short and fast race for solo and tandem boats. The slalom is a whitewater race in which quick turns test ease and accuracy of maneuverability. Contestants must make their way as quickly as possible through a course. Suspended poles make up the gates that must be navigated

in a certain order. Some gates must be approached in a downstream direction, while others must be undertaken by going upstream. Touching or missing a gate results in penalties to one's score.

For endurance athletes wishing to push themselves to the limit, participating in long-distance canoeing marathons is the perfect test. Found around the country, these races vary in both distance and degree of difficulty, but they always pose formidable challenges. One of the toughest is the AuSable River International Canoe Marathon, one of North America's most prestigious marathon canoe races. It is an annual 120-mile (193 km) race held in Michigan. Dating back to 1947, it is the longest nonstop canoe race in the country. Beginning at 9:00 P.M. one evening, teams of 2 paddle overnight for about 15 hours straight, stopping only to run while portaging

their canoes on their shoulders around 6 dams. They do not pause to eat or sleep, and they drink through hoses that allow them to keep paddling.

Canoes can also be used to experience the ultimate thrill of surfing ocean waves. **Outrigger canoes** were developed long ago by paddlers who wished to journey across the ocean in craft that could safely ride through swells and waves. Their solution was to attach an outrigger to a canoe. Today, outrigger canoeing is a popular recreational activity in Hawaii and an important part of Hawaiians' heritage. There are annual competitive events for canoe surfing, sprint, and marathon races. Most outrigger surfing events take place in huge surf with four to six people per canoe.

Just Add Water

One of the best things about
canoeing is that many different
people can enjoy it and participate.
No matter your age or ability level,
from beginners to experts, there is
an activity to fit. Many children get
their first canoeing experience during
a family vacation or summer camp.
It is an activity that the whole family
can enjoy together. It's a great way to
experience the outdoors and be active
at the same time. Nature lovers

OPPOSITE: Canoeing allows family members or friends to share an
adventure together in one boat

appreciate the beauty and serenity of gliding along a still lake. Athletes and risk-seekers can get the exercise and challenge they desire.

Some people canoe to experience quiet and solitude. Nature photographers take the opportunity to get close to nature and wildlife. From a canoe, they can soak up the scenery and see things they never would from shore. Other people use canoes when fishing or to hold their gear on camping trips. Adrenaline junkies appreciate canoeing for the thrill and challenge it provides, the rush of excitement they crave. Most canoeists take part for fun, but there is also a large group of people who favor the competitive side. Racing against one another and the clock is their biggest motivation.

There are a large number of canoeing competitions each year throughout the U.S. One racing event is sprint canoeing, a classic test of speed and endurance. In long, specially designed boats, paddlers race in straight, divided lanes. Leaving one's lane is not allowed and results in the paddler's being disqualified. The categories are for single paddlers (known as C1), pairs (C2), and fours (C4).

Whitewater competition is composed of slalom and wildwater racing, both of which require extremely high levels of physical fitness, strength, and skill. Major slalom competitions are run on artificial courses where paddlers have to navigate their way through a series of gates as quickly as possible. On an artificial course, the water flow and obstacles remain the same for every paddler. Between rounds, the water flow can be adjusted and obstacles moved to vary the course. Wildwater races, on the other hand, are run on natural rivers. In wildwater, there are no gates. The only goal is to get down the river as fast as possible.

The Triple Crown of Canoe Racing is a trio of races held annually in North America. It recognizes the top performances by marathon canoe racers who compete in all three events. The General Clinton Canoe Regatta is a single-day, 70-mile (113 km) race in New York. Michigan's AuSable River Canoe Marathon covers 120 miles (193 km) nonstop. The third race, La Classique, is a 3-stage race of 124 miles (200 km) held in Quebec. Competitors in these races maintain a pace of 50 to 80

Individually or with a partner, Serge Corbin (pictured) of Quebec dominated the Triple Crown of Canoe Racing from its 1992 establishment until 2003, winning all 12 Triple Crown championships.

CANOEING

strokes per minute. These world-class races are popular spectator events, and they attract national and international attention.

Athletes who participate in these races need to be in excellent health. To reach the level of fitness needed, they put in many months—and sometimes years—of practice and training. They build their lungs and muscles to have the strength needed to keep paddling without tiring. Canoeing can be quite strenuous and hard on the body. Being in good physical condition will make canoeing easier and more enjoyable for everyone, not just athletes. Canoeing puts stress on a person's muscles, in particular the arms, shoulders, and back. It is important to warm up and stretch properly before any canoeing session.

Doing some fast walking or jogging will get blood pumping throughout a person's body. Certain stretches

Being in good physical condition will make canoeing easier and more enjoyable for everyone, not just athletes.

are especially beneficial for canoeists. Arm and shoulder muscles can be warmed up by practicing some swimming movements or paddle strokes. Reaching overhead and bending from side to side will stretch the torso. Stretching before and afterward can increase a person's range of motion and may reduce the risk of soreness and injury. While the arms and torso may do most of the work, the whole body is involved in canoeing. Competitive athletes train hard to become as fit as possible. Their efforts pay off with strong muscles and overall healthy bodies.

Along with physical conditioning, a canoeist also needs to develop mental skills. Out on the water, the ability to act quickly is necessary when maneuvering a boat and paddle. Especially in whitewater situations, canoeists need to learn how water moves, how to assess risk, and how to respond promptly. Important qualities for all paddlers are self-reliance and self-awareness regarding one's ability level. Quick reactions and wise decisions are critical to a person's physical safety. Any paddler attempting extreme stunts needs to keep a clear, calm head when deciding which actions are worth the risk.

There are many ways to get involved in the canoeing community. The American Canoe Association, the nation's largest paddlesport organization, has thousands of members and hundreds of clubs across the U.S. and abroad. These clubs and centers offer starter classes as the perfect introduction to canoeing for both adults and children. Instructional sessions are widely available and inexpensive. Beginners can get the knowledge and tips

Monster Journey

The record for the longest canoe trip ever taken is held by a father and son from Canada. It began in June 1980 when Don Starkell and his two sons, Dana and Jeff, portaged their canoe down the street from their home in Winnipeg to the shores of the Red River. Their goal was to paddle to Brazil via the Mississippi River, the Gulf of Mexico, and the Amazon and Orinoco rivers in South America. Jeff dropped out in Mexico. The men nearly starved and were shot at, robbed, and jailed along the way. But amazingly, Don and Dana made it. Two years and 12,181 miles (19,603 km) later, they reached their destination. Their epic voyage put them in the they need to take to the water. Canoeing is a great way for novice boaters to get on the water because it's easy to learn. Seasoned paddlers can get involved with tours and canoeing groups to find new and exciting places to paddle.

Once a person understands the basics of canoeing, the possibilities are vast. With a paddle in hand, you can gain access to exciting new places. Canoeing allows exploration of narrow rivers and streams as well as expansive lakes and seas. It is one extreme sport that almost everyone can enjoy in some way, and it draws enthusiasts from all walks of life. Places to launch are plentiful, and it is often not too difficult to find a paddling partner to share the journey. For challenging the elements and testing a person's endurance, canoeing can't be beat. For those with a spirit of adventure, it delivers both thrills and fun!

Glossary

adrenaline   a hormone produced by the adrenal glands to aid the body in meeting physical or emotional stress, characterized by increased blood flow and heightened excitement

amateurs   people who do something—such as a sport or hobby—for pleasure and not as a job; as non-experts, they lack the skills that professionals possess

carbon dating   a method used by scientists to determine the age of an object

dry bag   a waterproof bag used for storage, usually having a roll-top closing system

fiberglass   a material made from tiny glass fibers that is very strong but lightweight

flat-water   describing calm water that does not have waves or currents strong enough to affect a canoe; also called quiet water

hypothermia   a dangerous physical condition that results from a decrease in body temperature after exposure to a cold environment

open canoe   a canoe without a deck or cover to keep water out

outrigger canoes   canoes that have one or more support floats (known as outriggers) attached to one or both sides of the hull

paddlesports	recreational activities involving the use and enjoyment of canoes and kayaks
swamping	filling a boat with water to the point of sinking it
synthetic	describing a material that is not found in nature but created through chemical processes
whitewater	water that is turbulent enough to appear white and frothy

Selected Bibliography

Buchanan, Eugene, Jason Smith, and James Weir. *Ultimate Canoe & Kayak Adventures: 100 Extraordinary Paddling Experiences*. Chichester, UK: Wiley, 2012.

Gray, Daniel A. *Canoeing for Everyone: A Step-by-Step Guide to Selecting the Gear, Learning the Strokes, and Planning Your Trip*. Guilford, Conn.: Knack, 2009.

Hosford, Bill. *Wilderness Canoe Tripping*. Lakeville, Minn.: Ecopress, 2009.

Jacobson, Cliff. *Boundary Waters Canoe Camping*. Guilford, Conn.: Falcon Guides, 2012.

Mattos, Bill. *The Practical Handbook of Kayaking & Canoeing*. London: Southwater, 2006.

Westwood, Andrew. *Canoeing: The Essential Skills and Safety*. Beachburg, Ont.: Heliconia Press, 2007.

Websites

All about Canoeing

http://paddling.about.com/od/paddling101/a/All-About-Canoeing.htm

This website introduces a broad overview of canoeing in a simple format. Topics covered include types of canoeing, paddling techniques, gear and equipment, safety, and more.

A Smart Start for Paddlers

http://www.boatingsidekicks.com/smartstart800.htm

This interactive website presented by the American Canoe Association and the National Safe Boating Council guides users through an animated course of water safety tips and information for paddlers.

Note: Every effort has been made to ensure that any websites listed above were active at the time of publication. However, because of the nature of the internet, it is impossible to guarantee that these sites will remain active indefinitely or that their contents will not be altered.

Index